THE
UNDRAFTED

HIStory: An Athlete's Journey Through Athetics and Life After

Timothy Felton

ISBN: 1533206120
ISBN 13: 9781533206121
Library of Congress Control Number: 2016908399
CreateSpace Independent Publishing Platform
North Charleston, South Carolina

CONTENTS

THIS BOOK IS DEDICATED

To all of the student-athletes that have committed their lives to academics and athletics. If anyone knows the devotion and hard work it takes to manage both education and sports, it is you; I hope you achieve all of your goals and dreams. I want to encourage student-athletes to never give up and follow their purpose, passions, and dreams. I also would like to thank all of the teachers, coaches, and role models who have instructed and inspired me through the years. Their guidance and leadership is the gift that keeps on giving.

INTRODUCTION

Thank you for purchasing my book. I wrestled with the very idea of writing a book because I did not believe I was capable of writing a book. I always liked English when I was in school, but I was concerned about my writing style. I would always write the way I talked. I would also struggle with grammar, punctuation, and context. Over the years, this hindered me from writing a book. My friends and family would always tell me I needed to write books on marriage, family, and child-rearing. I considered their advice; but, when I sat down to begin writing, I realized my true passions were youth and sports. At that point, I decided to write a book that would help encourage student-athletes to maintain a balance between academics, athletics, and life afterwards. As a former student-athlete, I want to do everything I can to help student-athletes succeed in life.

I wanted this book to be a great book that people could find helpful. There are plenty of books written by great people with great stories, but I use to think writers were the only ones who wrote books. The more I thought about it the more I realized there is a book inside of everyone. Every college spring break I would visit my former high school, and I would always visit my defensive coordinator's social studies class. My former defensive coordinator would ask me to speak to his class and student-athletes about my college experience and being a student-athlete. On one occasion, there was a parent present as I addressed the class. After class ended, I sat down with the parent and her son, who was an athletic-student. Notice I said athletic-student. This young man was a great athlete but did not excel in the classroom. His mother was confused and frustrated with the fact her son had been offered several Division-I football scholarships but had to settle on a junior college because of his grades and low ACT scores. I shared my story of being recruited by Division-I colleges, not passing my ACT test, and having to attend a smaller college with the young man; which was similar to his story. This encounter later prompted me to start a non-profit organization to mentor student-athletes throughout the recruiting process.

I knew writing a book would allow me to share my journey with others. I wrote The Undrafted to help student-athletes recognize the importance of finding their passions and purpose, focusing on their academics, exhibiting perseverance and hard work, and never giving up on their dreams. My journey began on the playgrounds and football fields I played on as a child. I remember playing a game called "throw them up, blow them up." In this game, one player threw the football up in the air and whoever received the ball was tackled by the other players. This is how I learned how to dodge and avoid tacklers on the field. Later, I took my playground skills to an organized football team at the local Boys Club. This led to playing football on the high school and college levels and to having an opportunity to work out for a few National Football League (NFL) teams.

Because education is not mandatory or required on the playgrounds or at the little league level, many student-athletes have to learn from their own experiences. All football players in Missouri are eligible to and may participate in sports during their freshman year of high school, but each following year depends on the student-athlete's ability to maintain good grades or a certain grade point average. I encourage all student-athletes to focus more on their academics because athletics will one day come to an end. I hope this book will inspire others to find out what their gifts and passions are and to go after their dreams, and I hope they enjoy the stories in this book. For all of the young men and women out there, I pray this book will give them some hope. For the people who have known me throughout my journey, I would like to thank them for supporting me along the way.

THE CRASH

It was a dark, rainy night. Our family was traveling to Clarksdale, Mississippi. The car ride was quiet, and there was no music playing. The rain was coming down so hard on the windshield of the car it looked as if I was viewing it through a magnifying glass. I was in the back seat of my parent's car sound asleep along with my two sisters, but suddenly I was awakened by loud thunder. I woke up crying and asked my mother if I could climb up front with her and my father. Initially, my mother said no, but then she allowed me to sit up front. My two sisters sat in the back seat arguing about switching seats. My mother, in her soft spoken voice, told my sisters to stop fussing over seats and allowed my older sister to sit wherever she liked because she was the oldest.

Then, the unexpected happened. Our car was rear-ended by a RV in Tunica, Mississippi. The car spent in circles several times before stopping. After the car rested, I looked up, but my eyes refused to ad-just to the accident; it was total chaos around me. My father and one of my sisters were unconscious, and I noticed blood splattered across my father's white t-shirt. Next, I remember waiting in the hospital with my mother and my oldest sister. Only three-years-old at the time, I had no idea what was happening. It felt like I was in a dream. I just stood in the waiting room dazed and confused.

A few hours passed before the doctor came out to talk to my mother. The doctor said, "She didn't make it." I thought the doctor said he didn't make it; but, once I saw my father walk into the waiting room, I knew my sister had died in the car crash. She was only six years old at the time of her death. After the doctor made the announcement, my mom and dad broke down crying. Not knowing what to do, I began to cry because I saw my parents crying. My oldest sister was in the Intensive Care Unit (ICU).

Can you imagine one minute you are playing with your sister and the next her body is lying in front of you lifeless. To this day, I can still visualize seeing my sister lying in her casket as if she was asleep. When I touched her cold arm and she did not wake up, I was frightened. I kicked, screamed, and cried to get away from the casket. My sister's death had a long-lasting effect on me for the rest of my life. From that day forward, I never touched another dead body because it was such a traumatizing experience. Even though I often asked myself why I survived the crash, I was around the age of thirteen when I realized I survived the car crash because God had a plan and purpose for my life.

THE UNDRAFTED

For many players, the National Football League (NFL) draft is an exciting time. We put in hours of practice, watching film, and weight training, hoping to hear our names called before a large audience. This time was no different. I sat glued watching the NFL Draft in my college dorm room hoping to see my name scroll across the bottom of the screen. Rounds 1-6 were completed. Then the NFL Commissioner walked out to announce the final pick of the 1994 NFL Draft—"Mr. Irrelevant." This is the title bestowed upon the last pick of the draft each year. I watched intensely hoping I would be "Mr. Irrelevant." After the pick was announced, my dreams of playing in the NFL were suddenly over. I was not angry, upset, or disappointed because I truly believed things happened for a reason. The only hope I had was to be selected as an undrafted free agent.

I believed being a free agent would be a better alternative because I would get to pick the best opportunity for me. However, a week passed with no calls from any NFL teams. I immediately turned my focus to my academics, graduating, and life after athletics. Unlike most athletes, I had a "plan B."

Most players see football as a way out or as a means to take care of their families. Many college football players' dreams are to enter the draft and play in the NFL. The reality is only a small percentage of college athletes reach the NFL. My reasons for wanting to play in the

NFL were like most athletes: being able to buy my parents a house, payoff bills, and live a better life. However, I was not disheartened for not making it to the NFL because I was always encouraged to finish my education so that I could have something to fall back on if I did not make it to the NFL. Playing in the NFL would have meant the world to me, but I realized I had other gifts and skills that would lead me to success.

THE KICKOFF

1

The smell of freshly cut grass on the football field was an indicator the football season had arrived. It was a sizzling hot summer day in July; I was seven years old. As I stood with sweat dripping down both sides of my cheeks, I was excited it was the first day of practice. My love for football began at the age of five as I sat in front of our black and white floor model television. While watching the Dallas Cowboys and Pittsburgh Steelers in Super Bowl X, I developed a sincere love for the game—a love I was always happy to express.

The head coach of the Falcons, a little league football team, instructed the players to line up in a straight line across the field. The assistant coach told everyone to run the length of the football field; the top three finishers would be the team's starting running backs. When the whistle blew, I sprinted like an Olympic sprinter through the finish line. The assistant coach ran over to me and asked for my name. He then shouted, "We have found our running back!" That was the first time I realized my ability to run fast was a gift from God.

After practice, my older sister and I caught two buses to get back home. When we arrived home, I ran into the house looking for my mom and dad to tell them the good news. I found my dad lying on the couch asleep. I shook his arm to wake him up. As he turned over he said, "Boy what do you want? You know I have to go to work later."

I replied, "Dad! I am the fastest kid on our football team!" He responded, "That is good son," and went back to sleep. My mom overheard me telling my dad the good news. She told me she did not think I should play football because I was little and may get hurt.

Though this was one of the greatest days of my life, it suddenly appeared to be crumbling down. I pleaded with my mother to let me play and promised her I would not get hurt. She understood football was really important to me, so she allowed me to play.

On day two of football practice, I was ready to carry the football and to show my running back skills. After we warmed up and exercised, the coaches divided the players into two groups. To my dismay, I was placed with the defensive unit. I was disappointed because I thought I was going to be the next star running back. The assistant coach came over to me after he saw the disappointment on my face. He said, "Son, I want you to use your speed on defense to make plays." I decided to give it a try.

The football coach put me at nose guard. I felt like a kid on Christmas Day that had not received any toys. This was the first time in my life I had to learn how to overcome disappointment. Feeling angry, I decided I was going to make as many tackles as I could on defense. Each time the offense would try to run a play, I would beat the offensive linemen and make the tackle. I used my speed in every single play. The offensive coach got so frustrated that he yelled out, "Can somebody please block that kid!" After practice I noticed the head coach talking with our running backs. Two of the running backs' fathers were friends with the head coach, and the other running back was the coach's son. In that moment, I knew my chances of becoming the team's running back were slim to none. It was apparent there was favoritism on this team.

On the bus ride home, my sister informed me our dad needed to start taking me to practice. She told me she could not continue to catch two buses every day, and it would be hard for her to take me to practice when school began. This was yet another disappointment because I knew it would be a problem getting to football practice. My father would not be able to take me to football practice because he worked two jobs, and my mom never learned how to drive. The only option I had was to quit the football team. When I was eight years old, my uncle took me to another little league football organization, but their team was full. I would not receive another chance to play football until age ten. I was disappointed I could not play football, but I realized in life you have things that are controllable and things that are uncontrollable. This was one of those things I could not control.

When I turned ten, I attended the Boys Club in our neighborhood. The Boys Club was within walking distance of my house. My parents paid my membership and football fees, which allowed me to play as a Herbert Hoover Eagle. I was excited and knew this experience would be much different this time around. Because the Boys Club was in walking distance of my house, I was responsible for getting to practice every day. When I joined the football team, it was a surreal feeling. For two years, I had imagined being in this position and now it was a reality.

As summer practice began, I noticed our two running backs had gained weight. We were always a light team. Before the season, all teams had to weigh-in players. The running backs had to run extra laps to make the weight. They were the last two to cross the scale at the weigh-in. Because they both were overweight, they had to play on the heavy football team. On the bus ride back to the Boys Club, I sat behind our head coach. Half-way through the trip, our coach turned to me and said, "I'm moving you to running back this season." Finally, my dream of playing the running back position had come true. I was extremely happy for this opportunity, but I knew I would have to work hard. I worked to improve skills such as ball control, agility, making cuts and awareness, and I focused on my strength— my speed. Being a smaller running back, I used my speed to beat defenders. I made sure I knew my strengths and played to them. I also worked hard in drills, learned the plays, practiced catching the football out of the backfield, and improved my pass blocking skills.

We played two pre-season games that year. We won our first pre-season game, and our defense recorded a shutout. Our next opponent was against the four time Super Bowl Champs, the Mathews- Dickey Bulldogs. This was a big game for us because it would let us know where we stood in the upcoming season. The Bulldogs scheduled the game on a Friday night at their home field. It was a back and forth defensive game all night. After three quarters, there still was no score.

With one minute left in the game, our coach called a time out. Our defense had just stopped the Super Bowl Champs inside the red zone. During the timeout, our coach came into the huddle and said, "We will be able to run about three plays, so make them count." The coach then gave our quarterback the three plays. The coach pointed to me as he walked toward the sideline. I knew from the look on his face he called one of my plays. All I could think about was scoring a touchdown. With the ball on the 10 yard line, we had 90 yards to go for a touchdown. When the ball snapped, I took a jab step left, came back to my right, and as I turned the corner, all I could see was the end zone. I raced down the right side line. "Touch down!" The crowd erupted.

The referees gathered at the 50 yard line. The side line referee informed our coach I had stepped out of bounds at the 50 yard line. Our coach then called "34" counter pass. Our receiver ran right past the other team's corner back, and our quarterback hit our receiver in stride for the winning touchdown. We won 6-0. It was only a pre-season game, but it gave us hope for the upcoming season. It was one of the greatest feelings in the world.

As fall turned to winter, we improved each week. By the end of the season, we were 6-0 and headed to the Super Bowl Game. Guess who would be waiting in the wings? The Bulldogs, the former Super Bowl Champs we beat in pre-season. When we arrived at practice on the following Monday, our head coach called a team meeting in the gym.

When the coach walked into the gym, he had a sad look on his face. Our coach started out by saying what a great season we had and he was proud of what we had accomplished. Then he dropped a bombshell on us. He told the team the Junior Football League (JFL) had taken all six of our games away, and we would not be playing in the Super Bowl Game that year due to the forfeiting of games.

We later found out our middle linebacker had turned thirteen-years-old before the season and used a fake birth certificate for registration, which made him ineligible for the Super Bowl. After the season was over, I had seven months to decide my next move. I was upset and disappointed, and I was somewhat disgusted with football. Even though I initially did not want to play football anymore, I had football fever again by the summer. After much thought, I decided to take my talent to the Mathew-Dickey Boys Club. This was an easy decision for me. I just wanted to play football, and it did not matter who I played for. However, playing for a championship team made my decision a lot easier.

On the first day of practice with my new team, I stood with one of my neighborhood friends as we stretched. He was the star running back for the Super Bowl Champs. He was very athletic. Though he had great vision and great moves for a running back, he did not have great speed. He would always joke around in practice. One day he whispered in my ear, "Don't think you are going to come over here and take my spot." He was smiling when he said it, but I knew he was serious. I just smiled back at him and did not say a word. I believed actions spoke louder than words, and because we were from the "Show Me State," it was show time! The next day in practice, our head coach informed the team our star running back had broken his leg and would be out for the entire season. I felt bad for him but looked at his absence as an opportunity for me. During the third week of class, we received our equipment.

Mathew-Dickey had a drill called the "Bull Ring." All of the players on the team would form a circle, with one player inside of the circle. I believe the drill was created to show how tough a player was. I was the first player to enter the circle. Looking around the circle reminded me of a firing squad. The idea of the drill was to stand in the middle of the circle while the coach called a player on the outside of the circle to hit you as hard as he could. As I examined the circle, I made sure I knew where all of the big players were stationed. Something told me to attack every player instead of just standing in the middle of the circle and absorbing the punishment. After going up against five or six players, I joined the other players on the outside of the circle. It was a great feeling to hold my own in the "Bull Ring Drill." My willingness to work hard and compete at a higher level in practice landed me a spot on the team.

In our first regular season game, we won big. I scored two touchdowns. We went on to win our next four games. Our last game of the season was against our rival the Royal Knights. The game was packed with fans on both sides. The Knights came into the game with a 4-1 record. If they won the game, they would force a playoff game against us the following week. With a win or tie, we would go directly to the Super Bowl. The game was a hard fought defensive battle. We scored first and led 7-0 with the extra point. The Knights countered with a scoring drive of their own. The score remained 7-7 at halftime. The Knights received the second half kickoff, and the score remained tied after three quarters. With 1:15 left in the fourth quarter, the Knights scored but missed the extra point, which made the score 13-7.

After the kickoff, we received the football at the 30-yard line. Our quarter back then ran "34" cross buck. I took the handoff from our quarterback; the outside linebacker crashed down inside. I sprinted around the right corner, and it was a foot race between me and the safety. I outran the safety to the end zone. The score was tied 13-13 with thirty-eighty seconds left in the game. Our defense held the Knights on offense, and the game ended in a 13-13 tie.

Now it was time to prepare for the Super Bowl. This was my first time ever playing in the big game. The Second Place Bowl was as far as I had gone when I played for the Eagles. Our opponent in the Super Bowl was the Raiders. They were the Saturday Conference Champs. Leading up to the game, I was excited to be headed to my first Super Bowl. We practiced for three days and had two days to rest our bodies for the game, but I approached the Super Bowl game as if it was just another game.

The night before the game it snowed and the temperature was around thirty degrees. This was another defensive ballgame. Both teams had scouted each other throughout the season, but the weather was in favor of the Raiders. We depended on our speed, but our ground game was a non-factor in the snow and mud. The Raiders jumped out to a 13-0 led. Our quarterback connected with our wide receiver for our first score of the game. After the extra point, the score was 13-7. We got the ball back with around one minute left in the game. Our coach called a timeout and huddled the offense near our sideline. The Raiders' defense was lined up, and I noticed they were overloaded on the right side. Our coach called the play 34 counter. I knew it was impossible for me to get around to the right corner because they were overloaded on that side. On the snap of the ball, I took the handoff and burst through the four hole for a five yard gain. Our coach called a timeout, but this time he called 34 Power. I looked at the Raiders' defense, and now they were stacked on the inside. I got the handoff and burst around the right corner.

I ran as fast as I could, but the safety had the better angle and pushed me out of bounds. I felt like I was running in slow motion. With ten seconds to go and no time-outs left, we had just one last play. Our quarterback ran back to the huddle from the sideline, and I waited on the play call. He looked at me and said, "33." After leaving the huddle our fullback said, "Follow me." I examined the defense.

Our quarterback took the snap from the center and handed the ball to me. I followed our fullback through the hole, but the middle linebacker blitzed and grabbed my jersey. I tried to stiff arm him, but he held on while their outside linebacker helped him bring me to the ground. Lying on the cold muddy field, I watched the clock tick to zero. I felt the agony of defeat. I did not want to get off of the ground because I thought I let my team down. One of our offensive lineman grabbed me by my shoulder pads and pulled me off the ground. I then lined up to shake our opponents' hands feeling disappointed. But I held my head up high because I realized I left everything on the field. As I walked off of the field, something in my heart told me that this would not be my last football game. Even though many little league football players would never play high school football, I knew there would be many more games in my future.

FIRST QUARTER

2

I can remember looking out of the window of my middle school during my seventh period class. There stood the first predominantly Black high school west of the Mississippi River. This high school had one of the best high school football teams in the state and produced many great athletes. Every day around 3:00 p.m., the football team would conduct football practice. As I watched practice, I imagined myself standing in the exercise line next to some of the greatest athletes in the state of Missouri. My eyes lit up every time the team captains would fire up the team as they beat their thigh pads like they were drums. I knew I was more than ready to become a Sumner Bulldog.

My oldest sister took me to a few of their football games, and the games were amazing. The band would play as the cheerleaders would have the entire crowd rocking in the stands. I could never forget the incredible athletes on the field, as there were several athletes from Sumner that had gone on to play on the collegiate and professional levels. The football team was coached by two legendary coaches, and they both served as father figures and role models for many players, even for those that had fathers at home.

After watching the Class 5A State Championship games in 1982 and 1984, I envisioned myself wearing that maroon and white uniform. In August of 1985, my dream became a reality. I made the

Junior Varsity Football Team. During those days, we would have between 80-100 players tryout for the JV Football Team. There were so many players trying out for the team that the players had to share uniforms during tryouts. Nevertheless, I soon received a uniform of my own. When I received my uniform from our athletic director, it was one of the greatest feelings in the world. I felt like a soldier in the military receiving his uniform and stripes for the very first time.

The sense of pride and tradition was incredible at Sumner. It started as soon as you walked in the school. Our principal at the time would come on the intercom every morning and say, "Good morning family!" He also would welcome the staff and students with his favorite saying, "Sumner High School, a Proud Tradition of Excellence since 1875!"

I played wingback my freshmen year. We had three good running backs, two talented wide receivers, and a quarterback. The crazy thing about playing for a powerhouse high school football team is that you are not the only gifted player. When I talked to people about my high school football team, I would tell them we had three first strings. If someone was not performing on the field or went down with an injury, there were two other players behind them that could step right in and play.

The transition from little league football to high school football was different. My role as a freshman was to learn from the upper classmen. We ran the Wing-T Offense; our head coach learned the famous offense from Grambling State University's legendary college coach. It took time to learn the new offensive system, but working with the varsity players made the transition smoother. I learned how to be patient as a running back and allow the blocks to form. I also learned everyone on the high school level competed for the top spot in each position. High school football definitely moved at a much faster pace than little league football.

Going into the last game of the season, I played as a starting player for the first time during the season. I opened the game with a 50 yard touchdown run and a 25 yard run later in the game. We won the game 50-0. It felt like the old Junior Football League days. It was an amazing feeling to finish our season with a win.

We practiced a fun tradition at Sumner. When the JV football season would end, our varsity head coach would select a few JV players to bring on the varsity squad for playoff games. After the game, I was sitting in the visitor's locker room when the varsity coach walked into the locker room. He congratulated all of the players on having a great season. When he arrived at my locker, he said, "Tim, those were two nice touchdown runs you had today." I then thanked the coach. Before he walked away, he said, "I'm going to bring you up on the varsity squad for the playoff game." My eyes lit up, and I smiled like the joker on Batman. All I could think about was putting on that varsity uniform; I even hoped we would wear our disco pants. They were all silk pants, maroon in the front and white in the back. We wore them in our first playoff game. These were the most comfortable football pants I had ever worn. The material felt similar to track tights.

We went on to win our first playoff game, and the stage was set for the quarter finals game against Hazelwood Central and the number one running back in the country. Because we knocked Hazelwood Central out of the playoffs in 1982, the tension between the two teams could be cut with a knife. The game had turned into a playoff revival. We would later lose to Hazelwood Central in the quarter finals, but the experience I gained was priceless. The game seemed to be played in fast forward; it felt like I had skipped college and went straight to the NFL. Nevertheless, Hazelwood Central would go on to win the Class 5A State Championship that year. Though I was upset we lost the game, I knew I was only a freshman and had three more years to make it to the state championship.

I remember sitting at the lunch room table with a few of the track guys. They were talking about running track during the summer months. There were two track clubs. Athletes either ran for the Blues or the Knights. Most of the guys at the table said they were going to run for the Knights Track Club. I decided, I too, would run summer track for the Knights. Summer track was competitive because track athletes from all over the area would run on the same team. The coolest thing about summer track was that you received the opportunity to travel to different cities to compete against some of the best track athletes in the country. It was an amazing experience.

The Poplar Bluff Meet always stood out in particular. The track team was expected to arrive at the track meet around 8:00 a.m. When we arrived at the track, our track coach gave each athlete their events for the day. When he got to my name he said, "Tim, you're running the 200 meters today." This was my only event for the day. However, I checked the track schedule and noticed the 200 meter dash was not until 8:00 p.m.

By the time my race came around, I was not motivated to run. I was mentally and physically drained from sitting in the hot sun and not being able to eat made it even worse. We could only drink water. I finished third in my meet and finished fifth overall. After the track meet, the team boarded the bus.

When I stepped onto the bus, there was only one seat available; it was next to one of our coaches. I had already decided this would be my last track meet, but I wanted to find the right time to tell the coach. It was not that I looked at myself as a quitter; my heart was just not into summer track.

Ten miles into our trip home, I told the coach this would be my last track meet. The coach then asked me why I was giving up track. I told the coach I was not giving up track altogether. I explained to him I would still run track for my high school. I also told the coach I wanted to focus more on football. The track coach then asked me, "What high school do you plan on attending?" I informed the coach I attended Sumner High School and played as a running back on the football team. The track coach turned to me and said, "I think you should quit football and focus on track because you will never play running back for Sumner High School because they have too many talented athletes." He also told me to give it some thought over the next few days. Our next practice was not until the upcoming Tuesday, so I had forty-eight hours to think about my decision. However, I did not need forty-eight hours to decide what I was going to do.

Over the next two days, I washed my summer track uniform and put it in a bag. When Tuesday finally arrived, I walked to the track where we practiced. I walked over to our track coach and handed him the bag with my uniform. The coach asked me, "What's in the bag?" I then told him my uniform was in the bag. The track coach looked at me with a sense of disappointment. I told the track coach thanks for working with me that summer and walked out of the gate to head home. In my heart, I did not feel like I was a quitter; I believed I did the right thing. Even though I ran track all four years of high school to stay in shape for football, I never returned to summer track.

SECOND QUARTER

3

O n the first day of our two-a-day practices for the new season, I noticed some of our players were missing from practice. I asked a few of the players on the team what happened to the players that were missing. Our head coach then told everyone to huddle up for a brief team meeting before we took the practice field. Our coach explained to the team some of the guys that did not return to the team could not play this season due to their grades. Then it dawned on me the state had set new academic standards for student-athletes. The new ruling was every student-athlete had to maintain a 2.0 grade point average in order to participate in high school athletics. Though this average may have seemed easy to obtain, this was not the case for some urban city athletes. Looking back, the last quarter of my freshman year I had a 2.0 GPA, and I was almost ineligible to play during my sophomore season. After this scare, I applied myself in the classroom and became more focused on my academics.

After our team meeting, it was time for our first summer practice. Our first practice ran from 8:00 a.m. to 10:00 a.m., and our second practice was from 1:00 pm to 3:00 pm. We had our break from 10:00 a.m. to 12:30 p.m. Some of the players would go home during the break, and some would leave to get something to eat; then return to the school to relax until our second practice. Sometimes I would ride my bike home during the break, and other times I would just relax at the school. The two-a-day practices over the course of two weeks were the hardest practices, but the work we put in paid off in the end. The summer heat made these practices even harder. At times, I would be physically and mentally drained from practice; but I kept going because I had one goal in mind, which was to have an opportunity to fulfill one of my childhood dreams to play in the state championship.

The running back position was loaded with several talented players. The flanker position, my position, had four players in this spot. Toward the end of the school year, the four of us discussed who would play the flanker position. We had a senior, junior, and two sophomores at the position. In my mind, it was a no brainer. Giving the position to the senior and junior players just made sense to me. Our offense was designed to run the football 99.9 percent of the time, and we threw the football maybe once or twice a game. The other players just assumed I would be on JV again. As the conversation continued, I set a goal to make the varsity squad during my sophomore year. At the start of practice, our coach met with the offensive unit. This differed from little league football where the coach would say no one has a position. Coach had his depth chart penciled inside of his head, and he laid out the formation rope, which helped the offensive linemen with their timing drills. He called out the offensive line first. The next group was the wide receivers. When the wide receivers were called, I was placed in this group.

Our receiver coach that year played college football at the University of Missouri and professional football in the NFL. He also played football at Sumner High School. His knowledge of the game was incredible. He taught us how to run routes, how to use our hands to catch the ball, how to locate the football, and how to beat the defensive back off the line. He also taught us how to run while pumping our arms and reach out at the last moment before catching the ball. I think this drill was why I made the varsity squad my sophomore year. Every time the ball was thrown, I used the drill to make the catch. Our head coach also took notice during our passing drill session. As a wide receiver in our offense, you had to become an excellent blocker because of our running game. Standing at 5'6 and weighing only 140 pounds soaking wet did not make this an easy task. Therefore, I focused more on getting stronger and using my God-given speed. Another important thing I learned was to always listen and to do exactly what the coach asked me to do. It was easy for my coaches to coach me because I was a coachable player. You must always remain coachable if you want to improve.

However adolescents, like myself at that time, were often the target of criminal activity. At the beginning of my sophomore year, I was approached by a drug dealer who attended our high school. He offered me $5,000 to kill someone who had stolen some of his drugs. In 1986, $5,000 was like having $50,000, but I respectfully declined the offer. I told the drug dealer, "I am an athlete, not a killer." As I walked away, I wondered why he would not kill the young man himself because he was the one who had problems with the guy. Nevertheless, I learned some decisions in life you may not be able to recover from. If I would have accepted the offer, I could have gone to prison or even worse ended up dead; but, I knew my life was much more valuable than money.

My sophomore season I played second string wide receiver behind our best receiver. I also played on our kickoff team. This was another area where I decided to make the best of my opportunities. Every time the ball was kicked off, I decided I was going to be the first one down the field to make the tackle. The crazy thing about our kick off team was that we got a lot of work done. Our high powered offense averaged over fifty points a game, which meant we kicked off between seven or eight times per game, giving me seven or eight opportunities to make tackles. I used my speed to get to the first and second wedge of the kickoff return teams. Even though I was not a starting player, I still excelled on the football field. Besides, I knew I was only a sophomore and had two more years to have an opportunity to play as a starter.

We finished the regular season 10-1, with our only loss attributed to the state powerhouse, the Jefferson City Jays. We won our first round playoff game but lost in the second round to Hazelwood Central. After making the varsity team my sophomore year, I looked forward to my junior season. My junior varsity days were over, and now it was time to shine.

Right before school let out for the summer, our head coach called a few players to his office. When I walked into the coach's office, the coach introduced us to a man wearing a McDonald's uniform; I noticed his uniform was very different from the ones I previously had seen in McDonald's restaurants. Coach told us the man was a Sumner graduate and owned his own McDonald's restaurant. The owner told us he currently was hiring and was looking for a few students to hire for the summer months. He gave us an application to fill out and said one of his managers would get in contact with us.

Two weeks later, I received a call to come into work for an orientation at McDonald's. It was such a great feeling to have a job and to earn some money at the same time. My dad worked two jobs, but his money was spent on food, clothes, and shelter for the family. With the money I made working at McDonald's, I could save in case I needed some things throughout the school year. It also kept me from asking my dad for money I knew we really did not have. This new chapter of my life was liberating.

During the summer, I also had to work out to get ready for the upcoming football season. It was not an easy task, but it was something I had to do. Knowing junior year was probably the most important year in high school, I had to be ready for the challenge. Therefore, I changed my workout plans to fit my work schedule; because the owner of McDonald's previously played football for Sumner, he knew to schedule the football players' schedules around football camp. We worked the morning shift in the month of June and the evening shift in July and August, which made the transition smoother.

When football camp began that summer, our school enrollment had dropped, and we were dropped from Class 5A to Class 4A. This made us one of the top contenders to win the Class 4A crown. We had a special group of juniors and seniors that year, and it seemed everyone arrived to camp in shape. It was all business and no play! The players were focused on one thing in football camp—to work hard to win a state championship.

Our offensive line that year was big, which was led by our center (6'2/305), guards, (6'0/265 and 5'10/270), and tackles (6'0/260 and 6'4/225). All of our skill position players returned with the exception of our flanker. We added a talented backup quarterback and two running backs. Overall, we competed at a very high level in camp.

Our defensive line featured a 6'4/300 freshman nose guard (who played on the University of Alabama's 1992 National Championship Team and in the NFL). We had great linebackers as well. The secondary was led by two brothers (who also would later play in the NFL). We also picked up a transfer punter we called "Georgia" (we called him Georgia because he transferred from Georgia). There were also other guys on the team that transferred from California, Mississippi, North Carolina and Texas.

During football camp, I was handed the punt return and kickoff return duties. I also played the backup flanker position. This particular football camp was special because everyone could just sense something great was going to happen in the upcoming season. I was more than ready for the challenge.

THIRD QUARTER

4

As we posted scores of 50-0, 45-0, 56-6, 74-6, 50-6, 58-0, 42-6, 46-0 and 90-0 in the new season, the newspaper headlines read, "Sumner Should Be Head of Class 4A." Area football fans and coaches were all saying we had the state championship already wrapped up, but our coach would not allow us to fall into this trap. He told us our first priority was to focus on the regular season and the Public High League crown. He knew Class 4A was just as tough as Class 5A. He also knew it always would be challenging to win a state championship on any level.

With us scoring points the way we did, it gave me the opportunity to run the football more. I even started in our second game against Roosevelt High School. It felt good to contribute to the success of our team. I was scoring touchdowns and making an impact on special teams. But in our week five game, something unfortunate happened. Our starting corner back went down with a leg injury. Usually, we would have one or two guys that would step right in to fill the spot, but we did not have depth at this position because of the new academic rules. When practice rolled around the next week, we were short one corner back. As I ran timing drills with the offense, our defensive coordinator coach yelled down to our offensive coach, "I need a corner back down here!" Our offensive coach then asked, "Who do you want?" To my surprise the coach said, "Send me Tim." In my mind

I said, "No, I'M A RUNNING BACK!" But in my heart, I knew it was the right thing to do. Therefore, I jogged down to the other end of the field where the defense practiced. I had played free safety at the little league level, so playing in the secondary was not a new experience for me.

Our defensive coach and the guys on defense welcomed me with open arms, but they told me I needed to understand the defensive focus now that I was on defense. Our linebackers spearheaded the defense. They were our Ray Lewis and Brian Bosworth of the defense. They actually used to call our middle linebacker Brian Bosworth. He even wore Brian Bosworth's jersey number (44), and he later attended the University of Oklahoma as well. Our free safety was the quarterback of the secondary while my track buddy played the other corner back position.

In the secondary, we played press man coverage every down. This was beneficial for the corners because of our size. We were short, but very fast, strong, and physical. We blitzed every time the opposing team quarterback dropped back to pass. Teams would try to pick on me at corner because I was the new kid on the block. Coach often would roll our free safety over to my side for help in the beginning. Once he realized I did not need any help, he kept our free safety in the middle of the field. With two shutdown corners on the field, it gave our free safety the opportunity to roam free. That year our free safety had nine interceptions.

Week after week, I was improving and learning more about the corner back position. Our secondary coach, another former Sumner football player, was a fundamental coach who taught us how to be aggressive and nasty on the field. Our other corner would always say, "Tim, you are the cover corner, and I am the knock-out corner." We could both cover and hit, but he would rather let you catch the ball, knocking the receiver and the ball into the water coolers. Coming from the offensive side of the ball, I would try to intercept every pass and score. I also used special teams as a means to score touchdowns. Occasionally, coach would use me on the offensive side of the ball, at flanker and the tailback position. Our quarterback told me one day in practice I was the first athlete at Sumner to play on both offense and defense in the same season. I never focused on being a two-way player. I just wanted to play wherever I could to help my team be successful. Being selfless is the best thing any athlete could do for their team because success has everything to do with teamwork. On the other hand, selfish athletes will always think about themselves or put themselves before their team.

By the end of our regular season, we were 9-0 and heading into the playoffs. In the first round of the playoffs, we beat Affton High School 44-6. During our time in rural Missouri for the playoffs, there was another great showdown scheduled to happen later that night: the Hillsboro High vs Dexter High game. We played at 1:30 p.m., so our coaches went to watch the game that night. Area fans could not wait for the Hillsboro-Sumner matchup in the Class 4A quarterfinals. Sumner had one of the best teams in the area, and Hillsboro had one of the best running backs in the state. However, the game never happened because 10-1 Dexter beat Hillsboro in a 48-41 shootout. At the time, Dexter's quarter back's passing performance ranked fifth-best in the national high school football history. He also ran for two touchdowns, which included the game winner with 1 minute left in the ball game. He later played at Oklahoma State University, completing sixteen of twenty-seven passes for 518 yards and five touchdowns.

That week in practice, we ran like we were Kentucky Derby race horses. Our coach told us all week to stay with our men and to not be heroes. I remember reading Dexter's coach and our coach's comments in the newspaper. Dexter's coach told the newspaper he had watched our defensive backs on film, and he knew we had better defensive backs then Hillsboro. Our head coach told the newspaper reporter our defensive backs had worked hard to prepare for this game and would be ready for the game. We were already a confident group, but those newspaper comments boosted our confidence to a higher level. The Sunday before the game, our team stayed in Sikeston, Missouri, about twenty miles from Dexter, because our coach usually arranged for us to spend the night to avoid the long bus ride the day of the game. On this particular game, we traveled to the game on the same day. While in Sikeston, we dined at the famous Lambert's Cafe, which is known for "Throwed Rolls." The restaurant served great food, and the hot butter rolls just melted in your mouth. Our stay in Sikeston was short but fun.

The forecast for the Monday night game showed rain. Our head coach had us bring both sets of our uniforms so that we could change into our other set of uniforms at halftime, if it rained. I thought it was a brilliant idea. Sure enough, it began to rain heavily on our way to the stadium. As we drove into the small town of Dexter, I saw a state trooper ahead of us directing us to the football stadium. This was not new for us as we would always have a state trooper guide us to stadiums when we would play in rural areas or small towns. The small town football games would all be the same. They would have banners of the high school football team, billboard signs, and little kids dressed in the team's apparel. The atmosphere in small towns was much greater than the atmosphere in large towns. When you sat on the sidelines, it felt like the fans were sitting right next to you. I can still hear the cow bells and air horns ringing in my ears.

As we entered the stadium that cold rainy Monday night, we were greeted by a host of Dexter fans. They were yelling profane language as we walked to our locker room. Our coaches had already given us instructions on how to handle these hostile situations, but for some reason this night seemed a little different. As we settled inside of the locker room, our head coach addressed us again on how to conduct ourselves on and off the field. Once the coaches left the locker room, our captains took the floor to speak to the team. After, one of our linebackers came over to the secondary guys and said, "Don't allow them to catch nothing tonight." These words sparked a fire in me to defend every pass thrown my way.

When we took the field for warms ups, we noticed the field was extremely wet. It had rained, but not for the field to be as wet as it was that night. After warm ups our team would always meet under the goal post for prayer. Our head coach and pastor would pray for our team, coaches, fans, referees, our bus ride home, and our opponents (we would also attend a church service at the pastor's church before the start of every football season). After the prayer, our head coach told us he found out the field was watered down before it rained. This was not anything new for us. We had been to other fields where the fields had been watered down. Teams did this to slow down our high powered offense. They were definitely threatened by our abilities.

Right before the coin toss, I remembered our head coach telling the captains if we win the toss, we wanted the ball to begin the second half. I was a little surprised our head coach did not want the ball first. In the playoff games, we usually received the open kickoff, scored, and put pressure on the other team's defense. For some reason, the head coach wanted to kickoff. Our defensive coordinator also dropped some weird news on the secondary players before we took the field. He told us we were going to play loose man-to-man coverage to start the ball game. We played press man coverage. This was kind of weird to hear coming from our defensive coordinator. He usually would turn us loose and let us play our usual style of play. But I trusted his judgment because they had scouted Dexter well.

On the opening kickoff, we pinned Dexter inside of the twenty yard line. When Dexter's quarterback broke the huddle and walked up to his center, I noticed he had a full mustache and beard. He looked like a grown man playing on a high school football team. The quarter back looked like he could have been an assistant coach. I was not intimidated by his appearance, but found it quite amusing.

During the first play of the drive, the quarterback hit his receiver on a quick post pattern for a first down. The crowd erupted, and the cow bells and horns were ringing; there was no time to set up because Dexter was going with a no huddle offense.

The footing on the field was horrible. Our defensive backs kept slipping, but Dexter never stopped firing the ball to their receivers. Before we knew it, Dexter was inside the ten yard line and threatening to score. By this point, I had missed two tackles and had given up three passes. Our defensive coordinator pulled me out of the game. The coach put in our freshman corner back who had returned from an early season leg injury. On the very next play, he slipped and gave up the game's first touchdown.

I told our secondary coach we needed to play press man coverage due to the field conditions. Our secondary coach conveyed that message to the defensive coordinator, and we switched back to press man coverage. Down 7-0, our offense responded. With the two point conversion, the score was 8-7. We shut down the Dexter offense for the rest of the first half.

Right before halftime, the rain picked up again. The rain was pouring down heavily as if someone was pouring buckets of water on us. Our uniforms were soaking wet, and we could not wait to get into the locker room to change into our other set of uniforms. When we approached the locker room door, we noticed the door was locked. As we waited on someone to come and unlock the door, the rain and wind was getting worse. By the time the guy came to open the locker room, we only had a minute before the start of the second half. Our head coach huddled us up in the locker room and told us we were not going to have time to change into our other uniforms because we had to get back on the field for the second half kickoff. I knew and everyone else on the team knew the guy with our locker room key was missing in action on purpose. I looked at this moment as just another hurdle of adversity we had to get over, and we did.

On the opening drive of the second half, our starting fullback went down with an ankle injury. To everyone's surprise, his backup came in and had a record setting game. He rushed for over 280 yards that game. For the rest of the game, our offense and defense were running on all cylinders. When the final horn sounded, the final score read Sumner 56, Dexter 13.

After the game, we dressed immediately and boarded our bus. As our bus pulled off, we heard items hitting the bus. Some of the Dexter fans and students were throwing rocks and plastic footballs at the bus. Our head coach told the bus driver to keep driving; he turned around and told the players to stay in their seats and not to respond. As I was sitting in my seat, I thought to myself, "Now this is too crazy!" I never thought a little game like football could affect people in this way. This was the first time I had experience racial tension. Nevertheless, I learned some people handle situations differently than others. Another situation soon would arise during the semi-final game against St. Clair High School.

With only four days to prepare for our matchup with St. Clair, our team focused on St. Clair's impressive running game and their star athlete as well. Going into the game, we knew we would have a good shot of winning the ballgame if we could stop their running game.

The weather was beautiful on game day. We received the opening kickoff and never looked back. At the end of four quarters, the final score was Sumner 36, St. Clair 6. After the game, there was no celebration because we knew we had one more game to win before we could celebrate. Now at 12-0 and heading to the state championship game, all we could think about was making history. Sumner had won state titles before, but no Sumner team had ever finished a season undefeated. With one game left, we had the chance to be the first Sumner team to reach this goal.

The state championship games in Missouri were played on the Friday and Saturday after Thanksgiving, so we spent our Thanksgiving with our coaches and teammates. That year the game was held at the University of Missouri. Our state opponent was the 12-0 Camdenton Lakers. Camdenton had a great offense and defense and was led by its outstanding quarterback and running back.

Camdenton won the coin toss and deferred to the second half. I remember our head coach telling our offense we were going to call three plays and run no huddle offense if we received the ball first. From the opening kickoff, I knew this was going to be a quiet ballgame. Throughout the season, our return team would either break the opening kickoff, or we would put our offense in a good field position. As the return guy, I would have the option to call return left or right. I would take three steps straight up the field and return the ball to whichever side I called the return to. This particular game, I called return left which was to our sideline. The kicker kicked a high kick; I fielded the ball on the ten yard line; and, I took my three steps straight up the field. As I made my cut to the left, I was drilled by a Camdenton offender at the fifteenth yard line. When the referee blew the whistle, our offense went no huddle. On our first play, the Camdenton's defensive end crushed our flanker. On play two, our flanker was hit for lose. On the third play, we went with our famous tailback reverse. Our tailback was hit so hard on the play he came off the field bleeding. I was standing on the sideline thinking to myself, "It's on today!"

On defense there was no difference. The first play from scrimmage, Camdenton's running back exploded through the hole for a first down. All I could remember was him running over one of our defensive lineman. He ran so hard he knocked off our lineman's helmet. As I watched the helmet spin on the turf, I knew it was going to be a battle. Before we knew it, we were down 8-0. Being down was not a big deal for us because we always fought back. The game went back and forth; by the end of the fourth quarter, the score was 16-14 Camdenton.

With the game on the line, we had the ball and were driving down the field for the go ahead score. It was 4th and 9, and our offense was on the move. Our head coach called a pass play for our flanker. He ran a ten and out pattern toward Camdenton's sideline. The catch was made, and it appeared to be enough for a first down. However, one of the referees came and spotted the football one yard short of the first down maker. Therefore, we had to turn the ball over to Camdenton with a few minutes left in the ballgame.

Our defense held Camdenton to only three yards on 1st and 2nd down. Our defensive coordinator called a timeout. In the huddle, he told us they were getting ready to run their option play. He gave everyone their assignments then left the huddle. When the ball snapped, Camdenton's quarterback sprinted to his right, our safety took the tailback, the quarterback faked the pitch, our linebacker took the fake, and the quarterback raced up the field all the way to the three yard line before being tackled by our outside linebacker. On the very next play, Camdenton scored, making the score 23-14 and ending the championship game. I remember sitting on our bench staring at the score board in disbelief. We were so close to winning the state championship and finishing the season undefeated.

Some players cried after the loss, but I did not. I was upset our seniors did not get a chance to go out on a good note, but I realized I had another year to get back to the state championship game. However, making it to the championship was no small feat. It took hard work, dedication, and team chemistry. What did I learn from the loss? I learned no matter how good you are there is always somebody better.

The bus ride home took only an hour and thirty minutes, but it felt like it took three or more hours. Some blaming occurred when we first got on the bus, but our head coach stood up and said, "We win as a team, and we lose as a team." Shortly after, the players either listened to their music or went to sleep. Once I got home, my focus shifted to preparing for the upcoming track season. For me, it was not the time for a pity party; it was time to go to work and get better.

The summer of my senior season was about all work and no play. I spent the summer conditioning, lifting weights, and working on my defensive back skills. I would run around Fairground Park every day to build my endurance. The park was located in one of the most dangerous areas in St. Louis. One day I remember finishing my run, going home, and turning on the 5 o'clock news. A young man had been shot minutes after I left the park. Thankful to be unharmed, I decided I was going to be one of the best defensive backs in the area that year. I was determined to meet this goal.

FOURTH QUARTER

5

With thirteen starters lost to graduation from the previous year's 12-1 team, it would seem likely that our team would be in the process of rebuilding. However, we did not rebuild at Sumner; we reloaded every year. The strong junior class we had the year before was now a senior class, so we returned ten seniors. We opened the season with a loss to the Class 5A powerhouse Jefferson City but went on to win our next nine games.

One of my best games during my senior year of high school came in week nine, the game we played against Soldan High School. During this game, I was the second leading scorer on the team even though I played corner back. Overall, I scored twice and had a safety. My first score came in the first quarter. I picked up a fumble and raced seventy-five yards for a touchdown; and right before halftime I sacked the quarterback in the end zone for a safety. Late in the fourth quarter, I intercepted a pass and ran it back seventy-five yards for another score. We won the game 60-6 and eventually went on to win our last ball game of the season, which made us 9-1 as we headed into the playoffs.

In the first round of the playoffs, we defeated Affton High School 20-0. In the quarterfinals, we beat St. Charles West High School 22-10, which set up a semi-final match against Webster Groves High School. Webster Groves came into the game with a record of 8-3 and with a

20-6 upset victory over 10-1 Potosi. We were expected to play Potosi in the semi-final game. They were one of the top teams in the state that year, and we even scouted them the whole year. When our head coach met with the team before our practice for the Webster Groves game, he gave us the scouting report on the team and reminded us they were as good as Potosi. He then told us we should not take any team for granted. Once again I trusted our coaches and scouting team. I followed Potosi's progress all season long, and I was sure we would meet up with them in the semi-final game.

The weather for the week was filled with rain, so we had to practice inside of our basketball gym at least three times that week. Our head coach even attempted to get the game moved to Lindenwood College, which had a turf field we could use, because he knew the O'Fallon Tech Field would be full of mud. However, we could not get the field at Lindenwood College for the semi-final game. When we did our walk through on the field at O'Fallon Tech, it was extremely muddy just as the coach expected. We won the toss and elected to receive the football, and we marched down the field for our first score on our opening drive. With the two-point conversion, the score was 8-0. We stopped Webster on their first possession. We got the ball back and scored again then received our two-point conversion. Now the score was 16-0, with our fullback scoring both of our touchdowns that day. The score remained 16-0 at the half. Webster scored twice in the second half to cut the lead to 16-14. We had numerous chances to score and put the game away, but we just did not capitalize on those opportunities. It was an intense defensive battle until there were fifty seconds left in the football game.

After we fumbled the football, Webster received the ball and drove down the field, but our defense battled back. We forced Webster into a 4th and 17 from our 31 yard line. I remember Webster calling a timeout soon after. Our defensive coordinator came into the huddle and said, "We are going to run our cover three defense because they are going to try a Hail Mary Pass." The team prepared for the next stage of our battle.

As Webster broke their huddle, I could see I had a tight end line up to my side. They split three receivers to the other side of the field. As the ball snapped, I dropped into my third of the field. I saw their quarterback drop back to pass; next, I saw our nose guard beat his man on the inside. At this point, he appeared as if he was on his way for the sack, but the Webster lineman grabbed our nose guard. However, no flag was called. My eyes shifted to the other side of the field, and I could see Webster running a three man route. Then one of our defensive backs slipped, and Webster's receiver ran past him and dove into the end zone for the winning touchdown. The extra point brought the score to 21-16, with only forty-four seconds left in the game.

As we waited for Webster to kickoff, our two defensive linemen both pointed to me and said, "Follow us and run this kick back for a touchdown." I called return left to the back wall unit. Webster kicked off then I filled the kick and followed my two linemen after breaking the first wedge of defenders, but I was tackled near mid-field. As I exited the field, I went to sit on the track behind our bench because I could not bear to watch the final seconds of the game. Our only hope was a Hail Mary Pass, but it was nearly impossible with the weather conditions. Besides, Webster was in their prevent defense which further complicated the game. We attempted to score but fell short. I was devastated and heartbroken once I realized we were not going to win the ballgame.

Next, I remember walking across the muddy field to shake hands with the opposing team. I knew one player from the Webster squad because he and I grew up together. He also attended Sumner before transferring to Webster Groves. He and I were the last two players on our teams to shake hands. When we met at mid-field, instead of a hand shake, he gave me a hug; then slightly shook his head. I could tell he really did not know what to say, so I just told him good game and wished the team good luck in the state championship. Webster Groves eventually went on to beat Kansas City Center 26-6 in the state championship game. Still to this day, my friend reminds me of their victory every time he sees me. Nevertheless, I went on to receive All-City, All-Public High League and All-Metro honors in football after completing the season.

The Webster loss was a little different for me than our state championship loss because this game was the last high school football game I ever played. During this time, I realized some players only played little league football and never played in high school; some would not play in college; and, many would never play on the professional level. My goal was to continue my football career and education in college. I had already achieved great things, and I was determined to achieve more.

I received letters from and was recruited by University of Iowa, University of Michigan, Oklahoma State University, University of Kentucky, Southwest Missouri State University, Emporia State University and Illinois State University; but, there was one obstacle standing in my way: the ACT Test. At the time, athletes needed to score a 15 or higher on the ACT test to be eligible to play Division I and Division II college football.

My counselor signed me up for the December ACT Test at Washington University, but I still needed to convince my dad I needed twenty dollars to take the test. Both my mom and dad had to drop out of school to work and help their parents. My mom dropped out in the tenth grade, and my dad dropped out earlier in the eighth. Being that they were from Arkansas and Mississippi, most kids were expected to do the same during those times. However, my parents always pushed education for me and my two sisters. All three of us later graduated from college.

I could remember my dad telling me, "Son, you have only one time to take the ACT Test because we don't have money to keep paying to take a test." My dad believed all tests should be free, so knowing I had only one chance to take the test put added pressure on me to pass the test. As I sat in one of Washington University's lecture halls, waiting for the test to be administered, the outcome of the test began to weigh heavily on me. Though I was not afraid of taking tests like some people, I just wanted to do my best on the test because it determined my future.

After the Science, Reading, and English sections were over, it was now time to take the Math section. The instructor passed out a scrap paper to everyone. Once we were instructed to open our book and to begin the test, I realized I had not taken most of the math presented on the test. I looked at those forty problems and told the instructor, "I don't need any scrap paper." I practically guessed every answer on the math part. On the bus ride home, I thought back to my sophomore year in high school when my counselor met with me in her office. She asked me if I would like to be placed in the college prep program and told me I had the highest G.P.A in my class at the time. Instead of taking advantage of the program, I rejected the offer out of fear. There were several athletes in the college prep program, and all of them passed their ACT Test on the first try. My fear was that I would not be able to keep up with the college prep program and participate in athletics at the same time, because the college prep program and its teachers were highly demanding. Two weeks had passed since the test when my counselor called me into her office to discuss my test results. She told me I received a 13 on my ACT Test; I was only two points shy of the qualifying score, but I knew I would have passed my test if I had been in the college prep program.

Division- I colleges like University of Kentucky, University of Iowa, and Oklahoma State University withdrew after discovering I did not pass the ACT Test. All that was left was Emporia State, Illinois State, and Southwest Missouri State. Each school asked me to take the test again, but I knew that was not possible. My dad had already told me I had one shot at the test so by the time our signing date came around; I was unsigned and undecided on my football future. Since I had taken and passed the ASVAB (Military Test), I talked to my dad about my situation; he thought it would be a good idea to enter the military. I also talked to my track buddy who had decided to enter the Marines. His older brother was already enlisted in the Marines, so my friend gave me the Marine recruiter's phone number to start the recruitment process. I figured there was nothing to lose; the military provided a job, benefits, education, and travel. Deep down in my heart, however, I knew I wanted an opportunity to play football on the college level, but I did not know how it would happen.

During my military recruiting process, the recruiter made me feel like a part of the military family. He would pick up the recruits in his new car, take us out to eat, and just talk to us about the perks of the military life. It was sort of like being recruited as an athlete, much similar to the recruiting trips where universities would connect you with one of the athletes to show you the campus and the benefits of attending their university. I was content with going to the military but every time I would see someone I knew, they would ask me what college I planned to attend. Instead of telling them I was going to the military, I would say I was still undecided on my college choice. I did not plan to tell anyone I was going into the military. My plan was to just leave and let them find out from my parents.

One day in track practice, our sprint coach asked me about my college choice. I had heard from a few junior colleges by this time, but they all were so far from home. I told our sprint coach that I was going to attend Coffeyville Junior College in Kansas. Our free safety had signed with them the year before, but he had gotten red shirted his first year at Coffeyville. Our track coach also reminded me he was red shirted and told me I should go to school on a track scholarship at Lincoln University. His statement brought back memories of what my summer track coach said to me as I prepared to enter my sophomore year of high school.

I thought about attending Lincoln University for a moment, but I knew in my heart I did not want to run track in college. Most of our track athletes loved football more than they did track, and I felt the same way. A few days went by, and I had a second thought about attending Lincoln University. I thought of a plan to take the track scholarship to pay for college then walk on to the football team and quit track once I made the team. I told our track coach my plan, but he explained to me it would not be a wise move to make. He said his coaching connection with Lincoln would be over if I made a move like that. He also said if he set me up at Lincoln for track, the coach would expect me to run track only. My conversation with the coach definitely ended my plan.

Before I knew it, it was March, and graduation was soon approaching. I had been attending a church with my sisters, but this one particular Sunday the Pastor taught on "Blessings." After giving the message, the Pastor gave an altar call. I went up to the altar and gave my life to Christ, and on Easter Sunday I was baptized. About two weeks later, our head football coach called me and two other players that had not signed a letter of intent to play college football into his office. He told us Lindenwood College was starting a football program and wanted to know if we would be interested in playing for them. We had ten seniors that year. Five players signed with colleges, and two decided to enter the workforce, leaving me and two other players to take advantage of this amazing opportunity. The new head coach then left some paperwork for us to complete and to return to the college. I was so excited about this new blessing, and I owed it all to my faith in Christ.

I waited until the following week to call the recruiter about my new decision. When we finally spoke, I told the recruiter I would not be entering the Marines because I had received a football scholarship. You would have thought I was already in the military based on the recruiter's reaction. The recruiter began to raise his voice and said I had signed the papers and could not change my mind. Now what the recruiter did not know was my friend had already spoken with his brother concerning this matter. His brother explained to us as long as we had not been sworn in we could change our minds. I felt a little bad about backing out, but this was a dream come true for me. I apologized to the recruiter and thanked him for what he had done for me during the recruiting process. I then began to focus on my new future.

After graduation, I worked out six days a week to prepare for football camp. I met with our new coach, and he gave me a workout schedule for the summer. I followed the schedule and added some of my own workouts to the schedule. I was determined to go into camp in the best shape of my life and to make a great impression on the coaches.

I remember our defensive back coach in high school telling us, "If you're in shape, work hard, and remain coachable, you can play for any college in the country." After he made this statement, the light bulb in my head lit up. From that day forward, I knew if I did these things I would succeed no matter what obstacles were thrown my way. This gave me confidence to exceed my expectations and to play football on the next level.

A NEW SEASON

6

We all have been taught there are four seasons in a year: spring, summer, winter, and fall. However, there are other seasons in life: a New Season, My Season, and of course Due Season. I had outgrown my seasons for little league and high school football, so now it was time for "A New Season" in my life. I also had heard people say going to college was the best season in their lives; I wanted to experience the same.

Each time you begin a new season in your life, it should be a refreshing feeling. Think about when you were a kid and got a new toy. That was one of the happiest moments in your life. Going to college to play the game that I loved was definitely a refreshingly new season in my life.

When I first arrived at football camp, we had to check into our dorms. The football team lived together in an athletic dorm, which I thought was pretty cool. It even made us closer as a team. I roomed with my childhood friend; we attended elementary, middle, and high school together. Being only thirty minutes away from home was a plus because you could go home every weekend. I decided I was not going to go home every weekend, so I pretended like I was in college out of state. I only went home if our high school was playing a major football game and, of course, for the holidays and seasonal breaks (winter and spring).

The first day of football camp was our testing day. We had to run two miles while being timed. I ran two and a half miles throughout the summer, so I was ready for the two mile race. The defensive backs and wide receivers ran in the same group. When the whistle blew, I took off nice and easy. I was use to my track buddy running neck and neck with me, but I did not see him anywhere in sight. Instead, a receiver from Iowa and I led the group. I led for the first seven laps, but our receiver from Iowa took the lead on the last lap. He finished first, and I was second. After the race, he came over to me and said, "Nice run. I thought I was going to be running by myself." Then he went on to tell me he ran the mile and two mile meets for his high school. I figured he was a distance runner based on how he finished the race. By this time, my friend had walked over to compliment me on the run. I then asked him why he was not up front. My track buddy said, "To tell you the truth, I didn't work out at all this summer."

Day two of camp, things became a little more interesting. Our defensive coordinator, an old retired Parkway West High School Football Coach, addressed all of the defensive players. I could recall him saying we had twelve defensive backs, but only four starting players could play at a time. He called his starting defense, "The Black Defense." Afterwards, he called out four defensive linemen and linebackers, as well as two back corners. When I heard two black corners, I immediately ran onto the field to one of the corner back spots. As I ran onto the field, I invited my track buddy. He ran to the other corner back spot. The defensive coordinator then said, "This is my starting defense." He told all of the other players, the eleven players that ran onto the field must be leaders from winning programs. As I looked at the linebacker unit, I saw our three linebackers from Sumner; the five of us that started in high school were all starting on the college level. It was truly an amazing sight. However, the coach did remind each of us we could be replaced if we did not play well.

I knew what the five of us brought to the defensive unit, but I had no idea of what the other six starters would bring to the defense. In the secondary, my friend and I were grouped with two hard-hitting safeties. Our defensive back coach taught us how to play cover 2 and 3 zone defense. This was a little different from what we played in high school because we played man-to-man ninety-nine percent of the time.

The most amazing thing I could remember was that we had players from all over the country. I could remember reading about players from big cities in the USA Today newspaper. Their writers would always say some of the best players came from the big cities in states such as Florida, Texas, and Alabama. As we went through our drills, however, I noticed my footwork was far better than some of the players from the bigger football capitals of the world. I then realized it is not where you are from but what you do on the field that matters. Where we were from at this point didn't matter, it was all about business on the field.

The first year of the football program, we had to play a JV College schedule. We went 7-0 during our first season. I started at corner back all seven games and also played special teams. After the season, I knew in my heart I probably would not return to Lindenwood College for my sophomore season. I believed I could play on a higher level, so I worked really hard in the weight room and in the classroom during the off season. I received permission from my academic advisor to take twenty-one credit hours that spring semester. Most of the classes were in my major, which was journalism at the time. A basketball player I met from Riverview High School and I decided we were going to focus on our academics during the spring semester. We did not go home except for spring break, and we also researched colleges we considered transferring to in the upcoming fall. We were extremely dedicated.

We narrowed our choices down to Tennessee State University and Emporia State University. After completing our research, we decided to visit Emporia State University in Kansas. Emporia was about five and a half hours from St. Louis. My friend from Riverview asked one of his basketball teammates if he would drive us to Kansas. My childhood friend and roommate also made the trip, and we all pitched in on the gas to and from Kansas. Emporia State originally recruited me out of high school, but the coach gave his last two scholarships to the defensive lineman and wide receiver from my high school team. I called my two former high school teammates and told them I was thinking about transferring to Emporia, and I also told them about my upcoming visit.

Our former defensive lineman shared our conversation with the coach that recruited me in high school, and he set up the visit to Emporia State University. I met with the head and assistant coaches, along with the players. I then explained we played a JV schedule our first year at Lindenwood College. The assistant coach that recruited me informed me I would be eligible to play if I transferred to Emporia. My mind was already made up, but I definitely knew I would transfer schools when I learned I would not have to sit out a whole season. Later that evening, we visited the campus and dorms. We also played basketball in the school's gym and attended a basketball game. My experience at Emporia State University was great. It was a much larger university, and I received a great vibe about the culture of the campus during the basketball game we attended. I definitely planned to make Emporia, Kansas my new home.

The next morning we said our goodbyes and headed back to our college. On the way home, we were convinced we would be attending Emporia State University in the fall semester. The minute we returned to campus, my Riverview buddy and I completed and mailed our admission forms. All we had left to do was wait on our acceptance and financial award letters.

We decided not to tell anyone we were transferring because my roommate and I still had to finish spring football practice. By the time spring practice ended, we had received our information back from Emporia. We both were accepted into the university and would soon be moving from the NAIA level to Division II level. We just had to get through our goodbyes first.

I had a great spring practice and had earned my scholarship for the upcoming season. After spring practice was over, the head coach met with each player individually. He told me he was honored to have me on his team. As he talked, I knew I had to tell him I would not be returning to Lindenwood next season. When he finished, he asked me if I had anything I would like to say. I first thanked the coach for giving me an opportunity to play college football. Then I went on to tell the head coach I would be transferring to another college next fall. The coach asked me was there anything he could do to help me change my mind. I told the coach I was recruited by Emporia State out of high school and just thought it would be a better fit for me. The head coach understood, and he gave me his blessings and wished me good luck at Emporia. So, after one season, I transferred to Emporia State University.

I finished my last semester at Lindenwood College and prepared for my summer workout. During the summer months, former players from our high school would always return to our high school to lift weights and condition. We also would return to help the current players on the high school team. Giving back was just one of the many things instilled in us.

I was close friends with our former high school flanker and free safety players, and we would work out twice a day. Our flanker attended Southern University in Louisiana, and our free safety attended Coffeyville Junior College before signing with Oklahoma University. I remember the day our former flanker told us he could not play football anymore because of an irregular heartbeat. It was a devastating blow to him, and us, because he was an awesome athlete. After receiving this news, I became even more grateful for the God-given talents and opportunities that I had been so blessed to receive.

After our summer was over, it was time to head to football camp. I rode to football camp with our defensive lineman (he had his own car since we were in high school). When we arrived to football camp, it was pretty much the same routine as it was during my freshmen year. The main difference was there were bigger and better athletes on the team. At the team meeting, the head coach gave us our instructions for camp and the school year. At Emporia State, work-outs began at 5:00 am, and we could not take any classes after 1:00 pm. Because I was a walk-on on the team, my financial aid had to pay for my first semester of school. According to the rules for walk-ons, athletes had to play in three home games and two away games to earn a scholarship.

Out of sixteen defensive backs, I started at nickel back in the secondary. During football camp, I competed with a senior corner back, but I was confident I was the better corner back. At the end of each week and each scrimmage game, players would be graded on their performance. Grade sheets were posted outside of the football locker room. After our first scrimmage game, the starting corner back in front of me graded out with a score of 95%. My grade was 93%. After the second scrimmage, I scored 96%; the starter graded out at 98%. The more I improved the higher our starting corner back would score. Entering our Black and Gold Game, our defensive back coach informed us this scrimmage would decide our starters for the season. I was extremely focused the week of practice leading up to the Black and Gold Game. I finished the game with five tackles and two interceptions. I played in the first seven games before I received a call from the financial aid office. When I met with the financial aid representatives, they told me I did not receive one of the grants I applied for and owed $700 for the semester. Our coach informed me I could not play in the next game if I did not have the money paid by the upcoming Friday. I missed the game that week. The following Monday I had another meeting with the financial aid board. I told the board my parents did not have $700, and I asked if I could do work study to pay the balance. One of the board members informed me football players at Emporia could not do work study and play football at the same time.

Now, I was faced with yet another major decision in my life. I had no choice but to stop playing football. I missed the last three games of the season. By this time, I was upset and ready to go home, but I decided to finish out the semester. After football season was over, I began to look for another college to attend. This would be my third college in a year and a half. I narrowed my decision down to Oklahoma University, Kansas State University, Southern University and Southeast Missouri State University. I had former teammates who attended each of these universities, so I applied to each university and waited on a response. I received my paper work from Southeast Missouri State University first. My financial aid paid for my entire spring semester in full. I thought to myself, "SOUTHEAST HERE I COME!"

It was a cold winter Sunday in January as I rode the Greyhound Bus to my new school. When I arrived to Cape Girardeau, Missouri, one of our offensive linemen from high school who attended Southeast Missouri State University picked me up from the bus station. It looked more like an old service station instead of a bus station. I felt like I was in a ghost town when I first stepped off of the bus; I even expected a cowboy to ride by on his horse.

Because my childhood friend and I had a disagreement before we left Emporia State University, I shared a room with our former offensive lineman. When I arrived to the dorm room, I was greeted by my childhood friend. We spoke to each other and later talked things out. I think we both understood life was too short to hold on to grudges; our friendship was too valuable to end because of some craziness.

The next morning, I went to the registration office to pick up my class schedule. I began as a journalism student when I first entered college, but I decided to change my major after much thought. I could remember this one literature class I had at Emporia State. The professor was talking as if he was "Shakespeare." In that moment I realized I wanted to do something else for the rest of my life. So, I did some research and narrowed my decision down to two majors.

One was education and the other criminal justice. In my heart I knew I wanted to do something to help children; after reading both major descriptions, I chose criminal justice. As a teenager, I remembered going with one of my friends to visit his juvenile officer. The juvenile officer talked to my friend and showed concern for his life and well-being. I thought to myself, "Now that's something that I would like to do some day." In my lifetime, I had changed my career path for the third time. I started out as a young child wanting to be a plumber, which then changed to a journalist and now a juvenile officer. I realized in life you just have to follow your heart and your passion to find true happiness.

Later that day after my classes, we had a team meeting. Once again I was a walk-on and had to earn a football scholarship. SEMO had just moved up from Division II to Division I-AA. I had to sit out for the entire football season because I had just transferred from Emporia State. For the remainder of that spring, I continued to work hard in the classroom and lift weights and condition. In April of my sophomore year in college, my roommate came to me about a summer internship with the Division of Recreation back home. His brother was a summer camp supervisor for the Department of Parks and Recreation. I completed the application and was selected for the summer internship position. We worked from 8am-4pm, Monday-Friday, and the internship ran from June-July.

Though I would work out after work, my workouts were a little different that summer because I did not have to be in shape for football camp. I basically lifted weights and completed a lot of distance workouts. That fall I watched every home football game, but the games were painful to watch knowing I could not be out on the field to help my team. I could not wait to return to the football field.

January of that next year, I was eligible to participate in the team's off-season workout program. The football team conditioning was held at 6:00 am three days a week. This was not a problem for me because we ran at 5:00 am when I was at Emporia. During the morning workouts, I would make sure I was upfront in every drill. We were taught in high school to run as fast as we could, until we could not run anymore, and to go as hard as possible to finish the workouts at the end. I ran so fast in our drills that some of the current players would tell me to slow down. In my mind, there was no slowing down because I was a walk-on trying to earn a football scholarship.

After our off-season program was over, our strength and conditioning coach (who came from the University of Florida) gave us a running test. The test consisted of twenty-five yard sprints and four 100 yard sprints. The defensive backs' time for the test was one minute and sixty-five seconds. I ran the test in one minute and fifty-five seconds, which made our coach change our test time to one minute and fifty-five seconds. This was only a pre-test, so we had to run the test again during football camp that summer when we returned for our two-a-day summer football camp practices. At the end of our spring practice, we had our "Red and White Football Game". I entered spring camp behind a corner back from St. Clair, MO. We defeated his team in the semi-finals of the playoffs my senior year in high school. Our starting secondary players were all going to be seniors that year. Our other corner back was from Kansas City; the free safety was from St. Louis; and, our strong safety was from Florida. The corner back I was behind on the depth chart was a good athlete. The only difference I saw was that he would get beat deep on some pass plays, and he experienced trouble playing the ball when it was in the air. Other than that, we were pretty equal.

My mind was set on becoming the starting corner back, and I did not care if we had four seniors starting in the secondary. I could remember some of the players asking me what I was going to do when I received my chance to play. I used to tell them one of those corner back spots belonged to me. By the end of spring camp, I had accomplished this goal. I won the starting job at corner back and a full scholarship. Heading into the summer, I knew I would have to work harder than I ever did before to keep my starting spot. So, after working hard all summer to win my spot and as an intern for the Division of Recreation, it was time to head to our two-a-days camp.

On the first day of two-a-days, we had to complete our running test. This particular year many of the players came into camp in shape and prepared for the running test. I ran in the first group and blazed through the test in one minute and fifty seconds, five tenths of a second faster than my spring test time. I also ran a blazing 4.38 in the 40 yard dash test. Because most of the team arrived in shape, our head coach did not run us as much after our practices during the season. Overall, I had a pretty good season that year. I only gave up one touchdown the whole season, and my performance on the field earned me some recognition from NFL scouts. I also made our football team's All-Academic Team.

During the season, the football players would attend the local high school football games on Friday nights if we were not out of town for an away game. At one of the high school games during my junior year, I happened to sit with a couple of guys from my home town that did not play on our football team. The guys ended up getting into an argument with one of the local residents. One of the guys I was with at the football game said something to the other guy's girlfriend. I thought to myself, this is something that happens in middle school or high school, not in college.

As we walked back to the football dorm after the game, we noticed the young man from the game started shouting from a parking lot located across from the football stadium. The young man was about thirty to forty feet away from us. All I heard the young man say was, "What's up now!" The next thing I knew, shots were fired from the parking lot. I took cover behind a parked car. As the bullets hit the steps, I counted six shots in a row. My life flashed before me. I prayed and asked God to spare my life. My prayers were answered; and, after the sixth shot, I told my friend, "Let's go!" We took off running and did not stop until we reached the football dome. I was thankful to have escaped the gun fire that night and just glad the situation did not end tragically. That night I learned how important it is to watch the company you keep, but I would soon experience another close call.

During the winter break of my junior year in college, I spoke with one of our offensive linemen from high school. He was home for the winter break, and told me he was on his way to the bus station to head back to school in Ohio. I told him two of our other friends and I had a rental car and could take him back to school. Our offensive lineman told us he would pay for the gas, so we filled up the gas tank and hit the road for the six hour trip. We all shared the driving responsibilities on the trip, and we got our friend back to school safe and sound.

When we arrived back in St. Louis, it was snowing heavily. As we attempted to get off on our exit, the car began to slide up the ramp. As I pushed down on the break, the car continued to slide. Out of the corner of my eye, I could see an eighteen wheeler semi-truck. As we continued to slide, one of my friends told me to turn my wheel into the big patch of snow on my right side. I turned my wheel to the right and slid into the big patch of snow, and the car stopped immediately. We avoided sliding into the path of the semi-truck. My friend's quick thinking saved our lives that day. As I sat frightened, I looked like a deer caught in headlights; I froze as my heart skipped a beat. I was so relieved and thankful the small patch of snow brought the car to a stop.

Going into the spring practice of my senior year, I was the only senior in the secondary; but, we had a talented group of freshmen and sophomores from Florida, Memphis, Alabama and Texas. Our secondary coach selected me as the captain in the secondary, and I remember him telling me I would have to be the leader that year. He wanted me to be a vocal leader on the field, but I was more of a leader that led by action. I believed if I taught you what to do and you watched me demonstrate it, you could learn how to do it yourself. I led by example.

There were two very talented guys behind me at corner back, one from Texas and the other from Florida. I took them under my wings and taught them not only about the corner back position but also about various issues in life. I helped them with their classes and even completed their financial aid packages. Some people would not go the extra mile to lend a helping hand to others, but I was not wired that way. I always believed it was important to help others because I knew a day would come when I would need help from someone. Eventually, we closed out our spring practice with three sophomores and one senior starting in the secondary.

That summer I continued to work out to prepare for my senior season. I also returned to my summer job with the Division of Recreation for the last summer. As a Summer Camp Recreation Counselor/Supervisor, I experienced working with youth for the first time. It was a great experience because it allowed me to gain hands-on experience as I provided recreational activities for youth. Sometimes people choose majors or jobs that are not their true passions. Some even choose careers based on how much money they will make or because it is something their parents want them to do. I worked as a camp counselor for two summers and as a camp supervisor my last summer with the Division of Recreation simply because I enjoyed working with youth.

Something else interesting happened that summer. My friend from Southern University asked me to take him to a job fair held by Coca-Cola. The company was holding interviews at a local hotel. While sitting in the ballroom, one of the interviewers came over and asked me was I there to fill out an application and to interview. I told the lady I already had a job for the summer and I was there with one of my friends. The lady still handed me an application and said, "Just fill it out while you wait on your friend." I completed the application and a short interview. The interviewer told me they were hiring fifteen store reps for the summer.

Two weeks had passed when I received a call from the Coca-Cola Company. The lady from the job fair called and offered me the job.

I was totally shocked when I received the call. I also felt bad I got the job and my friend did not. However, I realized God gave me favor and the job was meant for me. I was definitely blessed because over 300 people had applied for the fifteen positions, so I took the job and worked until my recreation job started in June. I was assigned to three major grocery stores where I stocked shelves and put up displays. The work environment was great, and I basically worked alone. I received $1400 from Coca-Cola within a month and a half, and I later earned another $1600 from my recreation job that summer. That summer was the most draining summer I ever had, but I believed it was all well worth it.

Once football camp started that August, I was in the best shape of my life. During our Red and White Scrimmage Game, however, I collided with our tight end. As I lied on the field in pain, I was hoping I was not seriously hurt. Our trainers quickly ran onto the field to care for me. My right knee was swollen, so they carted me off of the field to the bench on the sideline. They immediately applied ice to my knee. After the scrimmage, I was given crutches to help me walk, and the young players were calling me "pops" and an old man. The head trainer told me he would schedule me an appointment to see our team doctor Monday morning and also told me to continue to apply ice throughout the night. I was afraid I had torn my ACL and would be out for the entire season.

Early Monday morning, a few other athletes and I rode in the team van to the hospital to visit the team doctor. Once we arrived at the hospital, the doctor took x-rays of my knee. I waited about twenty minutes for the doctor to return with the x-ray report. When the doctor came back into the room, he said: "I have good news. There is no major damage to the knee." I was very happy I did not have any major damage. The doctor then informed me the swelling should go down in a few days. Just as the doctor had said, the swelling went down after three days. I had some soreness in my knee at first, after about a week, my knee was fine. However, our secondary coach held me out of practice the week before our first game against Southwest Missouri State University.

Our second string corner back from Texas stepped in, and we did not miss a beat. Going into the game, I was not sure if I was going to start in the game because I had not practiced in two weeks. It was not until after our warm-ups before the game that I found out I was starting. Our secondary coach told our corner from Texas I could not lose my starting spot due to an injury. Our corner from Texas was slightly upset but still came over to me and said, "Let's go Felt! Have a good game."

The game against Southwest Missouri State was a fast-paced, hard-hitting game. Each team had good athletes on both sides of the ball. Right before halftime, a Southwest quarterback (who was a transfer from the University of Missouri) ran a quarterback bootleg to my side. I came up and made the tackle, but one of our linebackers tackled the quarterback from behind, which caused both of them to fall on top of me. I could remember my left foot being caught under them.

When they got off of me, I stayed down on the field. My left ankle was throbbing with pain. Once again our training staff had to help me off of the field. Once they carried me to our bench, they looked at my ankle and applied ice. As I sat on the bench, our defensive coordinator handed me the headset. On the other end was our secondary coach from the coach's box. He asked me if I was okay and could I play. I told the coach I would get my ankle taped and try to go back into the game. The trainer taped my ankle, and I jogged down our sideline; but, when I tried to back pedal, I could not. By this time, Southwest was driving the ball and completing passes all over our secondary. Our defensive coordinator handed me the headset once again. When I got on the headset this time, our secondary coach was yelling at the top of his voice. He said, "TIM, CAN YOU GO?" I told our coach I could not back pedal at all, which is the key thing for a corner back. I remember him saying a few profane words before I handed the headset back to our defensive coordinator.

If you were thinking things could not get any worse think again because they did. In the second half, my backup went out of the game with a back injury, and our strong safety and running back also were knocked out of the game. In the secondary, which was already thin, we were forced to play with two freshmen for the rest of the game. We lost the game 21-10.

On the bus ride back to the school, I iced my ankle. I knew the routine by now, back to the doctor on Monday. When I arrived at the doctor's office that Monday, I just felt something was not right with my ankle. The doctor took x-rays, and when he returned with the x-ray report this time, he said, "I have some bad news." This was definitely something I did not want to hear, especially as a senior. The doctor told me I had a torn ligament in my ankle. I then asked the doctor, "What does that mean?" The doctor told me I could choose to have surgery or see if my ankle would heal on its own. I told the doctor I did not want to have surgery, so the doctor gave me a prescription and put a brace on my ankle. He also said I would probably be out for about five weeks. I figured this would work out because I would still have six weeks left in the season to play.

When week five arrived, my ankle still had not healed. It took another three weeks for me to return to the field. Right when I was scheduled to return, our head coach called me in for a meeting. In the meeting, he offered me a chance to take a medical redshirt, which would have allowed me to play one more season. I told our coach I would have to decline the offer. I also told the coach my plan was to play the last two games of the season and graduate in May. Besides, my fiancé and I had already had two children, so another year of school definitely did not fit into my plans. Even though the coach said he would have loved for me to return for one more season, he also said he understood my situation.

My first game back we played Kentucky State at home. We won the game, and I had two interceptions. In my last college football game, we beat Tennessee State, and I had another interception. I only played in three games, but I finished the season with five interceptions. After the last game, I was sitting in the locker room when our coaches came around one-by-one to thank and congratulate each senior. It was a great feeling knowing we went out on a winning note, but it was hard to imagine this could be my last time ever playing football because the last two seasons had already been tough enough. My junior year we finished 2-9, and my senior year we finished 3-8. At the end of the season, I won the Ken Hager Award for being the Top Defensive Back my senior year. I was invited to participate in a regional combine camp in Atlanta at Georgia Tech University. I had two Pro-Day workouts with the Cleveland Browns and Indianapolis Colts. I also received invites to Canada, Arena League Teams and a team from Europe. Our fullback and I both were contacted by the team from Europe. The coach told us their season began in March, so it was decision time for me again because I was enrolled in my last twelve credit hours and was scheduled to graduate in May.

I decided to stay in school to graduate, but our fullback dropped his classes and headed over to Europe to play professional football. I talked to our fullback a few times while he was in Europe, and he told me I would have been a superstar if I would have played for Europe. He definitely was one. He even sent us newspaper clippings from Europe that read, "The American Nightmare." However, I received my last offer from the Calgary Stampeders. I spoke with my fiancé at the time about moving to Canada, but she informed me she did not want to move because our daughter would be entering kindergarten that year. Therefore, I decided to graduate and start my career because it was time to go to work and provide for my family.

During my last semester in college, I completed an Internship with the Department of Probation located in Cape Girardeau County, and I worked with adult offenders on probation with the court. Even though I did not plan on working with adult offenders, I believed the internship could be a resume builder, so I took advantage of every opportunity that would help me build my career. My professor from my law enforcement class even told me about an opportunity the Criminal Justice Department offered with the Division of Youth Services, and I later worked as a Juvenile Tracking Officer for one year. I was assigned to one juvenile offender, and I tracked his progress at school and home.

In May of 1994, I graduated from Southeast Missouri State University with a Bachelor of Science degree in Criminal Justice. Hearing my mom, dad, family and friends yell my name as I walked across the stage was priceless. After graduation I headed back to St. Louis and was prepared to enter the workforce. My fiancé and I were married in July of that year, and two years later my wife and I had our third daughter.

7

The Call

In June of 2002, I received a life-changing phone call. After the third ring of the telephone, I leaned over toward my night stand to answer the phone. On the other end of the phone was my younger sister (my parents had another daughter several years after losing my sister). I answered, "Hello." My baby sister said, "Tim, I have some bad news." My first thought was one of our parents had passed away. Her next words were, "They found Crystal at the bottom of a pool." Crystal was my oldest sister's daughter, my ten year old niece. The phone call seemed unreal. I thought to myself, this cannot be happening again. History cannot be repeating itself. I hung up the phone and sat frozen in my bed glaring at the ceiling with tears rolling down my face, crying silently on the outside but screaming on the inside. My wife turned to me and asked, "What happened?" I told her with my trembling voice, "They found Crystal at the bottom of a pool." The more questions my wife asked the more quiet the room became. I was in a daze.

I could not remember the name of the hospital or the area my younger sister had told me. My wife had to call her back to get the information. She immediately began to pray. After she prayed, she asked me, "Do you think we should go to the hospital?" I told my wife, "I'm going to wait until I hear back from my younger sister." A few minutes later, the phone rang. It was my younger sister. She informed me the family was heading to the hospital. By this time, my wife had gathered our children and said, "We need to head to the hospital."

As we headed to the car, my wife asked, "Would you like for me to drive?" I responded, "No, I'll drive." The drive was only about forty-five minutes, but it seemed like four hours. During the car ride, all I heard was my wife praying and my younger sister's voice saying, "found at the bottom of the pool." When we arrived at the hospital, we stopped at the information desk. The receptionist gave us my niece's room number. As the door opened, I could see my niece lying on a flat table covered up to her neck. Everyone in the room was praying, but I knew in my heart she was gone. I stood in the corner of the hospital room in shock and disbelief. I stayed as long as I could, but I eventually stormed out of the room. My wife followed me into the waiting room area of the hospital. I sat in the waiting room trying to be strong for the family, but it was extremely hard. About fifteen minutes later, my sister walked into the waiting room to share the bad news I dreaded to hear, "She's gone and in a better place now." She thanked the family for coming to the hospital for support and told us she would give us a call later. As we walked to our car, our kids begin to cry. My wife grabbed the car keys as I entered the passenger's side of the car. The ride back home was quicker than the ride to the hospital, but I fell asleep because I was both mentally and physically exhausted. When we arrived home, my wife prepared the kids for bed. I sat up most of the night staring at our bedroom walls envisioning my niece lying on the hospital table before falling asleep. I never imagined going through a tragedy like this a second time. However, moments like this one reminded me of the importance of continuing on because there is always life after tragedy.

8

Life after Athletics

If you would have asked me what I wanted to be when I grew up, I would have likely said a plumber or a sports writer. Even career days at school typically consisted of policemen, firemen, doctors and lawyers. Though I chose significantly different professions throughout my career, receiving opportunities to work in multiple aspects of the work force would have never crossed my mind as a child. Also, I would have never imagined myself as someone who ministered to and mentored hundreds of students and athletes.

My father was a custodian supervisor at Washington University and hoped I would get a good paying job or enter the military after high school. My mother, a daycare teacher and later a stay-at-home mom, just wanted me to be successful in life. My parents kept me grounded and encouraged throughout my life. I was inspired by my dad's work ethic and his dedication to working hard on two jobs for over twenty years. However, I decided to take a different approach and chose to attend college, graduate and work one job. I learned later in life you can work one main job and save, invest and supplement your income with other jobs you love.

There is life after athletics, but the transition from sports to a new career is an emotional transition for many athletes. Most student-athletes do not have a Plan B or backup plan. Because making life changing decisions can be emotionally challenging, the transition after athletics can sometimes cause athletes to enter a depressing stage in their lives. Some athletes even try to live out their unfulfilled dreams through their children. As a football coach, I have seen parents force their children to participate in sports. Just because a kid is 6'4, 300 pounds, it does not make him a football player. In high school, I remember a football player that was 6'6, 300 pounds but went to college on a music scholarship—a true example that size does not determine a person's talents. In all, acceptance is definitely the key to surviving the transition.

I had a few friends that actually beat the odds and made it to the NFL. When they each made it to the NFL, I was happy just to know someone I played with made it to the professional ranks; but, there also were people that were not as happy for their achievements. Included in this group of people was one of my friends.

He told me he was very upset he did not make it to the NFL, and he even found himself talking negatively about those who did. He later realized he struggled with his self-esteem and dignity. He did not believe he did everything he had set out to do in his athletic career, and he just could not let go of this belief. On the contrary, I knew how to let my athletic career go and transition into my next career.

My decision to stay in college and graduate instead of going to Europe or Canada to play football did not weigh heavily on me. Once I made my decision, I embraced my new journey in life. Some say the sky is the limit, but I believe you can set your own limits for your life. I am a true testament to this statement.

My first few jobs were at home. They were called household chores. I developed my work ethic from working around the house—cleaning up my room, washing dishes, taking out the trash and cutting grass.

This work ethic set the foundation for the hard work I experienced in football and ultimately life after football.

During my college days, I cut hair to make extra money. I learned my hair cutting skills from my dad as I often watched him cut my hair for years as a child. After college I decided to enroll in barber school mainly because people in college told me I should get my barber's license. After graduating from barber school, I cut hair in a barber shop part-time for two years. It was not a particular goal of mine, but anything I put my mind to became a reality.

After football, I applied for several youth service jobs, and I was hired as an intensive case worker with a children's home after completing three interviews. I provided direct care and supervision for older youths in a residential setting. In July of 1994, I received a call from one of my high school teammates. He was coaching a seven year old little league football team at Herbert Hoover Boys Club. This was ironic because I played football there as a child. He asked me if I would like to be an assistant coach, and I agreed to help him coach the team. This was my way of giving back to the sport that had given so much to me. I worked at the children's home for four months before receiving a job with the family court as a youth leader. In this position, I worked directly with youth in a detention center. After five years, I was promoted to Assistant Supervisor. In this position, I supervised a staff of twenty-one youth leaders. One year after my promotion, I was promoted to Deputy Juvenile Officer. My job as a juvenile officer involved the supervision of juveniles on probation. In November of that same year, I became the Youth Director at my church.

To help other student-athletes succeed in life, I formed the Youth Exposure Sports Foundation, Inc. Our mission is to make sure student-athletes have a balance between academics, athletics, and life after athletics. I further give back to others by volunteering my time and by mentoring through Big Brother/Big Sister programs and Presbyterian Children Services as well.

After sixteen years as a volunteer football coach, I received a call from another friend. He recently had been hired as a head football coach at a public high school. I was offered a job as the defensive backs' coach, and I coached for two seasons. After my second season, I decided to apply for a coaching position at an all-boys private high school. I emailed the new head coach my resume, and he called me in for an interview. I soon was hired as the new secondary coach.

Though I chose criminal justice as my major in college, education was a close second. Once I started coaching at the high school level, I had to obtain a teacher's certificate, and I later had an opportunity to serve as a teacher's assistant. I am currently working as a Case Manager/HiSET Administrator. I work with GED students ages 17-23. I conduct student orientations, assessments, success treatment programming, case management services and college tours. Because education is important and essential for success in any career field, I am dedicated to ensuring my students take full advantage of the opportunities education offers.

In all, life after athletics is not how I imagined, but I could not imagine it as any better. My goal was not to have a lucrative NFL contract but to become successful in life because I knew only a small percentage of players would make it to the professional ranks. For some, adjusting to life after athletics can be mentally exhausting. Student-athletes dedicate a majority of their time to preparing for the next level then suddenly their sports career is over. Thankfully, I was prepared for the transition and ready to embrace change in the next phase of my life. Though I competed in a Regional Combine and Pro-Day workouts, I was not fortunate enough to make it to the National Football League, but I did not want to return home and just sit on the corner and talk about how great I was in high school. I witnessed some of our greatest high school football players return home, start using drugs, become alcoholics and battle depression. For this reason, it is very important for student-athletes to understand their transition does not begin when their athletic career ends; it begins the first time they step on the field or court. We must see ourselves as successful from the beginning and discover our passions and purpose in life because each decision we make determines our life after.

THE CONCLUSION

My journey into my career after athletics did not start when my athletic career was over. I already knew my two passions were youth and sports, so my focus was not on trying to make it to the NFL. Instead, I just placed my focus on my life after athletics because life is just like football. Sometimes you will fumble, jump offside, get intercepted and you may even give up a score.

As a student-athlete in high school, I did just enough to get by in my education. I chose to remain in regular classes, and I even had to take Math 099 when I got to college because of my low ACT math scores. After I completed the course, I received a letter grade but no credit hours for the course. If I could do it all over again, I would have listened to my high school counselor and entered our College Prep Program.

Because of my past experiences, I encourage student-athletes to focus on their education (the word student is listed first for a reason). I also like to encourage student-athletes to find their gift, purpose, and passion in life. I realized at a very young age one of my gifts was the ability to run fast. This gift allowed me to play football at a higher level, an experience for which I am thankful. Later, I discovered my purpose was to work with youth, which coincided with my passion for youth and sports.

Student-athletes need to understand the transition from athletics can be difficult, but the transition can be smooth if you prepare yourself. If you are fortunate to play on the high school, college or professional level, you will realize transitions are all different. Transition was never a problem for me because I shifted my focus to my career. However, this process did not begin when my athletic career ended. It began once I realized my purpose in life.

My willingness to work hard, to be accountable, coachable and teachable, and to dedicate myself to my academics and the sport I loved created opportunities I would have never imagined. I wrote this book to encourage student-athletes to maintain a balance between academics, athletics and life afterwards, to always strive for excellence, and not to allow circumstances to dictate their futures because I am a true testament to a successful life after athletics. I will soon graduate with my Master's Degree in Human Services and hopefully will pursue my PhD (Doctor of Philosophy) Degree in the future. If you have given up on your dreams or have stopped dreaming, then I say to you, "Dream another dream, and pursue your passions and purpose." We each were placed here on this earth to make an impact; be sure to make yours count.

WARNING: Sports Without Education is Dangerous!

Sports Food for Thought:

> Many college football players will not be drafted by a NFL team.
> Many college men basketball players will not be drafted by a NBA team.
> Many high school baseball players will not be drafted by a MLB team.
> Many college ice hockey players will not be drafted by a NHL team.
> Many track athletes will not make it to the Olympics.

ODDS OF MAKING IT IN THE NFL

If you are lucky enough to be one of the 6.5% who become NCAA football players and one of the 1.5% of that group to make it to the NFL, you will be lucky to get THREE years out of it. At a minimum salary, you will not make enough to live on for the rest of your life.

WHAT IS GOING TO PROVIDE FOR YOU AND YOUR FAMILY AFTER FOOTBALL IS OVER?

Your College Education!

GLOSSARY

Football Terms

Backfield: The group of offensive players — the running back and quarterback — who line up behind the line of scrimmage.

Down: A period of action that starts when the ball is put into play and ends when the ball is ruled dead (meaning the play is completed). The offense gets four downs to advance the ball 10 yards. If it fails to do so, it must surrender the ball to the opponent, usually by punting on the fourth down.

Drive: The series of plays when the offense has the football, until it punts or scores and the other team gets possession of the ball.

End zone: A 10-yard-long area at each end of the field. You score a touchdown when you enter the end zone in control of the football. If you're tackled in your own end zone while in possession of the football, the other team gets a safety.

Extra point: A kick, worth one point, that's typically attempted after every touchdown (it's also known as the point after touchdown, or PAT). The ball is placed on either the 2-yard line (in the NFL) or the 3-yard line (in college and high school) and is generally kicked from inside the 10-yard line after being snapped to the holder. It must sail between the uprights and above the crossbar of the goalpost to be considered good.

Fair catch: When the player returning a punt waves his extended arm from side to side over his head. After signaling for a fair catch, a player can't run with the ball, and those attempting to tackle him can't touch him.

Field goal: A kick, worth three points, that can be attempted from anywhere on the field but is usually attempted within 40 yards of the goalpost. Like an extra point, a kick must sail above the crossbar and between the uprights of the goalpost to be ruled good.

Fumble: The act of losing possession of the ball while running with it or being tackled. Members of the offense and defense can recover a fumble. If the defense recovers the fumble, the fumble is called a turnover.

Handoff: The act of giving the ball to another player. Handoffs usually occur between the quarterback and a running back.

Hash marks: The lines on the center of the field that signify 1 yard on the field. Before every play, the ball is spotted between the hash marks or on the hash marks, depending on where the ball carrier was tackled on the preceding play.

Huddle: When the 11 players on the field come together to discuss strategy between plays. On offense, the quarterback relays the plays in the huddle.

Incompletion: A forward pass that falls to the ground because no receiver could catch it, or a pass that a receiver dropped or caught out of bounds.

Interception: A pass that's caught by a defensive player, ending the offense's possession of the ball.

Kickoff: A free kick (meaning the receiving team can't make an attempt to block it) that puts the ball into play. A kickoff is used at the start of the first and third quarters and after every touchdown and successful field goal.

Line of scrimmage: An imaginary line that extends from where the football is placed at the end of a play to both sides of the field. Neither the offense nor the defense can cross the line until the football is put in play again.

Offensive line: The human wall of five men who block for and protect the quarterback and ball carriers. Every line has a center (who snaps the ball), two guards, and two tackles.

Punt: A kick made when a player drops the ball and kicks it while it falls toward his foot. A punt is usually made on a fourth down when the offense must surrender possession of the ball to the defense because it couldn't advance 10 yards.

Red zone: The unofficial area from the 20-yard line to the opponent's goal line. Holding an opponent to a field goal in this area is considered a moral victory for the defense.

Return: The act of receiving a kick or punt and running toward the opponent's goal line with the intent of scoring or gaining significant yardage.

Rushing: To advance the ball by running, not passing. A running back is sometimes called a rusher.

Sack: When a defensive player tackles the quarterback behind the line of scrimmage for a loss of yardage.

Safety: A score, worth two points, that the defense earns by tackling an offensive player in possession of the ball in his own end zone.

Secondary: The four defensive players who defend against the pass and line up behind the linebackers and wide on the corners of the field opposite the receivers.

Snap: The action in which the ball is hiked (tossed between the legs) by the center to the quarterback, to the holder on a kick attempt, or to the punter. When the snap occurs, the ball is officially in play and action begins.

Special teams: The 22 players who are on the field during kicks and punts. These units have special players who return punts and kicks, as well as players who are experts at covering kicks and punts.

Touchdown: A score, worth six points, that occurs when a player in possession of the ball crosses the plane of the opponent's goal line, when a player catches the ball while in the opponent's end zone, or when a defensive player recovers a loose ball in the opponent's end zone.

Football for Dummies (USA Edition)

ACKNOWLEDGMENTS

There have been so many people who have been instrumental in my life, personally and professionally, that deserve recognition. Unfortunately, to mention everyone I would have to write another book. I would first like to give thanks to my Lord and Savior Jesus Christ for creating me and for giving me life more abundantly and favor. I would like to thank my parents, my wife Athina, children Kina, Tichina and Sarina, immediate and extended family, friends and teachers, Pastors David and Nicole Crank, Richard and Pricellious J. Burruss, and Gregory and Joanie Purnell. I would also like to thank all of my coaches throughout my playing career: Coach Victor, Robert Smith, Anthony Hood, Lawrence Walls, Richard Perry, Arnold Sams, David Schroeder, Larry Kramer, John Mumford and David Dumars. To my editors Erica L. James, Hamza Khalid and Cindy OHara. Graphic Designer Peter Okomota, thank you for bringing my book to life. Last but not least, thanks to all of my teammates over the years for competing with me and pushing me to excellence.